7.76

J
954.98
Bhu

Bhutan

Children of the World

Bhutan

For their help in the preparation of *Children of the World: Bhutan*, the editors gratefully thank: Employment and Immigration Canada, Ottawa, Ont.; the US Immigration and Naturalization Service, Washington, DC; the United States Department of State, Bureau of Public Affairs, Office of Public Communication, Washington, DC, for unencumbered use of material in the public domain; Ugyen Doje, Dechen Lipman, and other members of the mission of the Kingdom of Bhutan to the United Nations; and Pratul Pathak, Milwaukee, WI.

Library of Congress Cataloging-in-Publication Data

Bhutan/photography by Yoshio Komatsu.
        p. cm. — (Children of the world)
    Bibliography: p.
    Includes index.
    Summary: Describes the home, family, school, customs, beliefs and rituals, and day-to-day activities of eleven-year-old Tinley living in Bhutan's capital city of Thimphu.
    ISBN 1-555-32892-X. ISBN 1-555-32867-9 (lib. bdg.)
    1. Bhutan—Social life and customs—Juvenile literature.
2. Children—Bhutan—Juvenile literature. [1. Bhutan—Social life and customs. 2. Family life—Bhutan.] I. Komatsu, Yoshio, ill.
II. Series: Children of the world (Milwaukee, Wis.)
DS491.7.B48 1988
779'.995498—dc19   88-21051

North American edition first published in 1988 by

Gareth Stevens, Inc.
7317 West Green Tree Road
Milwaukee, Wisconsin 53223, USA

This work was originally published in shortened form consisting of section I only. Photographs and original text copyright © 1986 by Yoshio Komatsu. First and originally published by Kaisei-sha Publishing Co., Ltd., Tokyo. World English rights arranged with Kaisei-sha Publishing Co., Ltd. through Japan Foreign-Rights Centre.

Copyright this format © 1988 by Gareth Stevens, Inc. Additional material and maps copyright © 1988 by Gareth Stevens, Inc.

Typeset by Zahn-Klicka-Hill, Milwaukee.
Map design: Sheri Gibbs.

1 2 3 4 5 6 7 8 9 93 92 91 90 89 88

Children of the World
Bhutan

Photography by
Yoshio Kamatsu

Edited by
David K. Wright,
MaryLee Knowlton, &
Scott Enk

Gareth Stevens Publishing
Milwaukee

. . . a note about *Children of the World:*

The children of the world live in fishing towns, Arctic regions, and urban centers, on islands and in mountain valleys, on sheep ranches and fruit farms. This series follows one child in each country through the pattern of his or her life. Candid photographs show the children with their families, at school, at play, and in their communities. The text describes the dreams of the children and, often through their own words, tells how they see themselves and their lives.

Each book also explores events that are unique to the country in which the child lives, including festivals, religious ceremonies, and national holidays. The *Children of the World* series does more than tell about foreign countries. It introduces the children of each country and shows readers what it is like to be a child in that country.

. . . and about *Bhutan:*

Eleven-year-old Tinley lives in Thimphu, Bhutan's capital city. Tinley and his family are Buddhists, and their lives are enriched by the rituals and beliefs of their religion. Only one in five Bhutanese goes to school, and Tinley is one of the lucky ones. He is becoming an expert archer in the Bhutanese style.

To enhance this book's value in libraries and classrooms, comprehensive reference sections include up-to-date data about Bhutan's geography, demographics, currency, education, culture, industry, and natural resources. *Bhutan* also features a bibliography, research topics, activity projects, and discussions of such subjects as Thimphu, the country's history, political system, ethnic and religious composition, and language.

The living conditions and experiences of children in Bhutan vary tremendously according to economic, environmental, and ethnic circumstances. The reference sections help bring to life for young readers the diversity and richness of the culture and heritage of Bhutan. Of particular interest are discussions of the historical background of Bhutan and of its geographical and political relationship to the neighboring giants India and China.

CONTENTS

Tinley's family: Phuntsok, Nawan, Tinley, and Sonam.

Tinley and his sister visit their little brother, Kenzan, at the temple in Sikkim.

LIVING IN BHUTAN:
Tinley, a Boy of the Himalayas

"Kuzuzhangpo!" says Tinley Lendhup Dorze. "Hello!" Tinley is an 11-year-old-boy from Bhutan. He lives with his father, Sonam, mother, Phuntsok, and nine-year-old sister, Nawan Zogal, in Thimphu, the capital of the Kingdom of Bhutan. Tinley's eight-year-old brother, Kenzan Rinzan, lives in Sikkim, an Indian state next to Bhutan. He is studying to be a Buddhist monk.

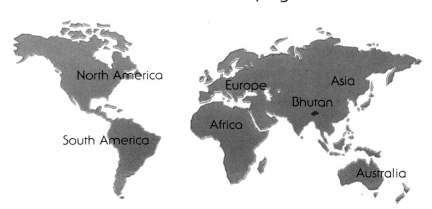

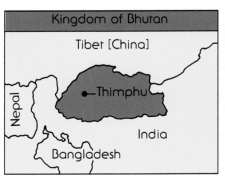

Tinley's house and yard. The family raises vegetables in the yard.

The nation's name, Bhutan, comes from *bhotanta,* an ancient Sanskrit word meaning "the very end of Tibet." Its name in Bhutanese is *Druk Jul,* which means "country of the dragon." It is a mountainous country. The Himalayas, which can be seen in the east, are the world's highest mountains. The people make what use they can of the mountains. Rice fields, or paddies, dot the mountainsides. Tinley's family grows food in their yard.

Rice paddies dot the mountainsides.

Thimphu, Bhutan's capital city.

Most people in Bhutan lead simple lives on farms and in forests. Because Tinley and his family live in Bhutan's biggest city, they have more modern things than many Bhutanese do.

But Tinley's family has one important thing in common with most Bhutanese, whether they are rich or poor. They are Buddhists. For three-quarters of Bhutan's people, the religion of Buddha is the center of their lives.

The Himalayan Mountains can be seen from eastern Bhutan. Tibet lies beyond the mountains.

Tinley's mother was born here in the Kur-choo Valley.

9

Tinley's father works for the government. His office is in a building in front of the great *Tachicho-Dzong*. The Tachicho-Dzong is the headquarters of Bhutan's government. Buddhist monks also live there. The Tachicho-Dzong was built as a home and school for monks.

Tinley's father works in these government buildings.

Tinley's father wears a *Kamni* over one shoulder. This piece of cloth is part of his daily dress, much like a necktie here.

The Tachicho-Dzong.

10

Tinley is named after three great monks.

The family built this altar in memory of Tinley's godfather.

Tinley always wears his amulet.

Buddhism Every Day

Buddhism for the Bhutanese begins at birth. Tinley was given his name by his godfather, a Buddhist monk named Dulup Top Rinpotche. When Tinley's godfather died, Tinley was given one of Dulup Top Rinpotche's beaded strings. Tinley wears the string as an amulet, or charm. He says that the amulet not only helps him stay calm and protects him from danger but also makes him feel powerful.

Every morning Tinley fills the water bowls on his family's altar. In the evening he empties them.

Tibetan Buddhism, also called Lamaism, is Bhutan's national religion. Everywhere in the country you can see monks in their red robes. They live in castle-like *dzongs*. The religious Bhutanese take care of their needs. People come to the monks for help with writing letters, planning farm work, building a house, or even predicting the future. Usually the second son becomes a monk. In poor families several sons may train to be monks.

Every village has its own temple, and each home has its own prayer room. *Dechen*, or Buddhist holy writings, are printed on flags. Pictures of Buddha, called *Thangkha*, are everywhere, especially at festival times.

Flags with Dechen.

A Thangkha at a festival.

Inside a dzong.

Reading a prayer.

Tinley and his father at morning prayer.

Buddhism also affects how people treat animals. Buddhists in Bhutan and Tibet believe that living beings carry the soul of someone who lived in the past and that the souls of those living now will enter the bodies of others in the future. So people hate harming any living thing. Many do not eat meat.

All Buddhists begin the day with prayer. They use beads to count their prayers. Then they study Buddhist scriptures. Tinley does not know them well yet, but he will. Sometimes monks come to his home to perform ceremonies.

Tinley's father is a religious man.

1. He joins his hands over his head.

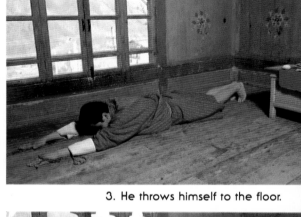

3. He throws himself to the floor.

2. He kneels.

4. He joins his hands over his head.

In prayer, people touch the floor with their foreheads. Tinley's father has a mark on his forehead from touching the floor every day for many years. The mark is a sign that he is deeply religious.

5. He touches his forehead to the floor.

Prayer and scripture wheels, called *Mani* wheels.

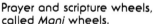

Inside the dzong of Tinley's mother's childhood.

Pictures of hell.

Family and guests eat breakfast on the floor.

After prayers, Tinley is ready for breakfast. His aunt, uncle, and two cousins are visiting his family, so the house is full of activity. Breakfast is a dish of rice and a cup of salty buttered tea.

After breakfast the men leave the house. Tinley's uncle must make a phone call. Phones are rare in Bhutan, only one for each 100 people. The one Tinley's family uses is outdoors. On the way back everyone stops at the small post office to catch up on the news of their neighbors.

Bhutan police officers.

An outdoor phone.

At the post office.

Tinley keeps his clothes in a closet. Clothes and shoes are hard to come by in Bhutan, so people take care of them.

Tinley makes sure his pleats are straight.

Cream protects his skin from the sun.

Time for school! Putting on his school uniform, a *goh*, takes Tinley some time. The goh is like a bathrobe or a Japanese kimono. Bhutanese men and boys wear it. They make pleats at the back and tuck it above the knee. Its front fold is a pocket that carries plates, knives, and other small things.

Tinley keeps his shoes well polished.

Women and girls wear a *kira*, which is a long, colorful piece of cloth. They wrap the kira around themselves like a long jumper and fasten it with a button at the shoulder.

Waiting for the school bus.

A Bhutanese School Day

Tinley's bus picks him up at eight o'clock. The Lunten-Yampa Junior High School is only a few minutes from his house.

Tinley knows he is lucky to go to a good school. Many of Bhutan's rural children do not go to school. Although education has become more available in the past 20 years, only one child in five goes to school.

The bus is popular. Few Bhutanese have cars.

The school grounds. In the distance is a monument to a popular king.

Lunten-Yampa Junior High School has 600 students from kindergarten through 10th grade. From the playground you can see all of Thimphu.

The children begin the school day by singing Bhutan's national anthem. Then they get in lines according to grade. Tinley follows the sixth-grade line into the building.

The children in their uniforms.

Tinley and a friend share a Dzongkha textbook.

Lendlup Dorze, the Dzongkha teacher.

New vocabulary words for tomorrow.

Tinley's first class today is Dzongkha, Bhutan's official language. Though Dzongkha is Bhutan's official language, the Bhutanese speak many others, too, like English, Nepali, and Schachopka, a language of eastern Bhutan. Tinley and his schoolmates often hear these three languages, as well as Dzongkha, on Bhutanese radio.

Tinley's homeroom classmates with their teacher, Pratima Devdas, from India. She is standing in the back with the children. Mrs. Devdas is assisted by two young people from Bhutan who are training to be teachers.

Classes last 40 minutes with five-minute breaks in between.

Tinley and his classmates study math, science, geography, history, Buddhism, English, and Dzongkha. Students and teachers use books written in English. Classes are also taught in English. With so many chances to use English each day, it has become Tinley's favorite subject.

After three morning classes, the students take a half-hour break for tea and cookies. The children must bring their own teacups from home if they want tea. People in Bhutan usually eat only two meals a day — one in the morning and one in the evening.

After tea break comes recess. The girls jump rope, and the boys joke and run around. Time passes quickly. Soon it is time to line up for afternoon classes.

A Dzongkha textbook.

Tea time! The children are hungry and ready for a break.

Prayers end the school day.

Until recently, monasteries served as schools. Even though Bhutan has had schools for over 20 years now, it will be some time before schools have everything they need. They are often short of teachers, so many teachers come from India and Bangladesh. Even today, only one out of ten people in Bhutan can read and write in any language.

Afternoon classes are over by two o'clock. After their last class, students meet in the gymnasium for prayer services led by teachers and older students.

One day Tinley will be one of the older boys leading the school in prayer.

A Walk Through Thimphu

Most of Tinley's schoolmates live at home. Students at rural schools often come from homes far away, so their schools have dormitories and cafeterias. Many Bhutanese rural children do not go to school because their parents need them to help with chores and to take care of younger brothers and sisters.

School begins in March and ends in November. Children go to school six days a week, Mondays through Saturdays. For those children who live near a school, education is free.

The shops in Thimphu have signs in several languages. These are in English and Dzongkha.

The only regularly scheduled bus is the one that takes Tinley to school in the morning. In the afternoon, he walks home through downtown Thimphu. It's a 30-minute walk. Tinley starts out from school with his friends, dropping them off along the way as they reach their homes.

Thimphu's main street runs along the Thimphu River. By law, buildings must be built in Bhutanese style, so the town does not have any modern-looking buildings. All of Thimphu's buildings have Bhutanese decorations.

Thimphu has been the year-round capital of Bhutan since 1962. Before then, it was Bhutan's winter capital. When Bhutan's king decided to put the capital there, not many people lived in the Thimphu Valley. Today over 20,000 people live and work in the area.

Until 1974, when the present king was crowned, Bhutan was closed to outsiders and quite isolated from the rest of the world. Yet because the schools are run in English, most children in Thimphu and many in the rural areas are fluent in the language. Travelers to Bhutan are often amazed when children run up to them in the street and ask, "Are you from San Francisco?"

Tinley strolls down a street in Thimphu.

A Mani wheel in a Thimphu street-corner shrine.

Thimphu does not have traffic signals, so police officers direct traffic at the crossings.

Bhutan's economy has been based on each family. The family grows or makes only what it needs for its own use or to trade for what it cannot grow or make. Today the country is more in touch with other countries and their products. Aid programs from other countries provide goods and services that Bhutan does not have. Australia provides trucks and Great Britain has provided mobile post offices. Other countries offer technical training to Bhutanese students. The government of Bhutan supports students who study in the United States, Australia, New Zealand, India, and Singapore.

On his way home, Tinley stops to see what one of the movie theaters is showing. Movies are popular in Bhutan, since there are not too many other forms of entertainment. Fewer than one in 100 people have radios, and there are few television sets. Most of the movies shown in Bhutan come from India, but some are from the United States. The movie theaters are always crowded.

At Thimphu's biggest gas station, people must pump their gas by hand.

A mailbox looks like a giant fire hydrant.

The children pass two monks on their way home.

Thimphu's movie theaters show three movies a day.

Home Again!

When Tinley gets home from school, he finds his mother at work at her loom. In Bhutan the women and girls make all the cloth for the family's clothes. Tinley's mother began weaving when she was just five years old. She is an excellent weaver, with a pattern only she knows. Each family has its own design, handed down from one generation of women to the next. No one else knows this pattern.

Today she is weaving a kira. To make a kira, she weaves three sheets of long, narrow cloth and joins them to make one sheet. It will take her more than two years to finish this kira. She uses silk threads of many colors to weave cloth picturing the flowers of her homeland. The national flower, the rhododendron, is a part of many Bhutanese patterns.

In Bhutan the mother, not the father, is the head of the family. The oldest daughter usually becomes the head of the household when her mother dies. Tinley's sister, Nawan, will inherit her family's house.

The family pattern.

The rhododendron.

Part of the new kira.

Tinley helps by spooling thread.

Weaving is delicate work.

Adjusting the border.

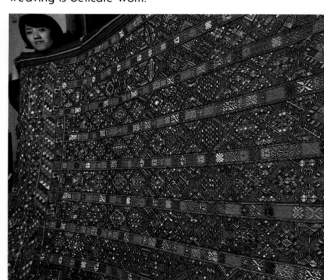
This kira took almost three years to make.

A rhododendron and kiras.

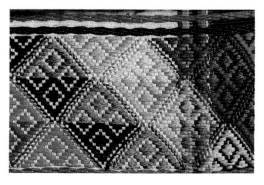

33

Tinley shoots a marble off his finger.

Many Bhutanese grow most of their own food.

Tinley, his family, and other Bhutanese people tend to be gentle, calm, and polite to others. For many centuries, the Bhutanese have lived with nature in richly wooded areas. But a quiet change has been taking place. The government is opening the country little by little to people and ideas from outside Bhutan.

Factories are being built. Schools are opening for more children. Modern schools and factories are big changes for a country where most people do not go to school or work outside their homes.

Tinley, at 11, has little idea of how much Bhutan is changing as he grows up. He still lives in a family which, like other Bhutanese families, does not have a family name. As the children of his generation grow up, they will find a different world. They will decide what will happen to their customs and beliefs as the outside world moves into Bhutan, and as they move out into the world.

Tinley likes to do his homework near his family rather than alone at his desk. He likes to study but doesn't know what he will do when he grows up. His mother hopes he will have a better life than many Bhutanese children have had in the past.

Tinley and Nawan do their homework together.

Cousins and neighbors do their homework while Tinley's mother weaves.

Tinley's school supplies.

Tinley practices his writing.

Tinley eats with guests from his mother's hometown.

Dinner for Family and Guests

The main food in Tinley's house is rice. Two kinds are popular in Bhutan: red and white. Many Bhutanese prefer red because they believe it gives them power.

Himalaya seeds — a little bitter.

Boiling rice in the temple for the monks.

No meat is wasted.

Rice with dried yak and pepper.

Rice with fish, vegetables, asparagus, and salad.

Tonight Tinley and his family have guests. Before dinner they pick up a handful of rice and knead it with their finger to clean their hands. At dinner they sit cross-legged. When eating, they hold the rice in one hand, dip it in soup from a side dish, and eat the rice.

Bhutanese cooking uses all kinds of peppers as the main ingredient. Every household has various dried and pickled peppers.

Salty buttered tea comes with all meals.

Bhutan's national dish is *ema-datzy*. *Ema* means "pepper," and *datzy* means "cheese." It is a spicy blend of yak cheese and boiled peppers.

A young servant cooks in a monastery.

Thrashing rice.

Peppers drying.

The Tsesey Bazaar in Thimphu is a place to shop — and talk.

The Tsesey Bazaar — Market and Meeting Place

Every Sunday brings the Tsesey Bazaar along the Thimphu River. *Tsesey* means "vegetable." Originally, only vegetables were sold here. But today vendors sell bamboo baskets, bows, and other things used in everyday life — even Western clothes.

This is because of the leader of Bhutan's Buddhists. He is the Dalai Lama, a man from Tibet who has been exiled to India by the Chinese government. Western charities send clothing to him in India, much more than he needs. His followers sell the Western clothing in bazaars like this throughout Bhutan, India, and Nepal.

But vegetables are still the market's main items. People bring different kinds of vegetables and edible wild plants to the market. Long-lasting vegetables like potatoes, onions, and cabbages are also sold in ordinary shops. But fresh greens, wild plants, and homemade cheese can be bought only at the Sunday bazaars. Most people buy their week's supply of food there.

Tinley and his mother go to the bazaar early in the morning because the best vegetables sell out early. The bazaar is crowded with whole families who come to visit and to help carry everything home.

Two boy monks visit with their mother in the marketplace.
They will return to the dzong at the end of the day.

Ripening tomatoes.

These days Tinley's mother and most other Bhutanese bring money to the market to pay for what they want. For centuries, Bhutanese people never used money as we know it. They just bartered, or traded, with each other when they needed something. Bhutan did not have its own money until 1974. Bhutan's people are getting used to the idea of earning and spending money instead of bartering.

Prices are not decided in advance in the Tsesey Bazaar. Buyers and sellers haggle until they reach a price both can accept. Since haggling can mean lower — or higher — prices, everyone is serious about shopping.

A shopper in a colorful kira.

"Try some dried yak meat!"

Bamboo baskets from southern Bhutan.

Weighing vegetables.

Persimmons are an autumn fruit.

Cheese is made from yak's milk.

Radishes and apples.

Bungchus are sold in pairs.

People bring bags and boxes from home, since the merchants at the bazaar don't supply them. Many carry a *bungchu* or two. The bungchu is an everyday necessity. It can be used as a lunch box, a basket, a plate, or a purse. Its mesh weave is so fine that it can even be used to draw water.

River weed for cooking.

Rice — the main crop.

Prickly ash seeds for seasoning.

A day's shopping.

Rain can't stop an archery match — not much can in Bhutan!

Bhutan's National Sport — Archery

When Tinley is not at home or at school, you can probably find him at an archery match. He loves the competition.

Bhutanese males are terrific archers. They will hold matches between two friends or two villages. Large crowds of friends and relatives come to cheer. In matches for adults, the rules are complicated, but children's matches use simple rules.

Selecting an arrow.

Tinley's a good archer, serious and strong.

The Bhutanese bow and arrows are made with bamboo. Bamboo from southern Bhutan makes excellent bows.

In classical, or Bhutanese, archery, archers aim above the spot they want to hit so that the arrow flies in an arc. Bhutan is a heavily wooded country where game cannot always be seen well in the woods, so classical archery is well suited to the land.

In 1984, Bhutan sent an archery team to the Olympics for the first time. They lost because of the difference in archery styles. Western archers aim directly at targets with powerful bows. For the Bhutanese archers, the targets were too close!

Tinley practices hard. He dreams of someday making Bhutan's archery team and taking his talents to the Olympics.

Bird feathers are attached to bamboo arrows with lacquer.

Archery targets get a lot of use.

Playing with a little cousin is a perfect way to take a break from studying.

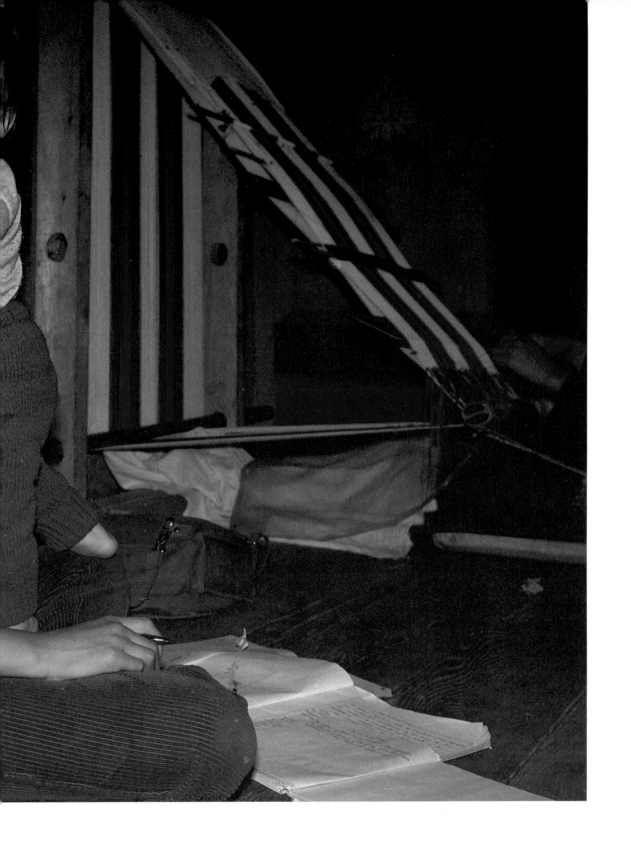

FOR YOUR INFORMATION: Bhutan

Official Name: Kingdom of Bhutan
Druk-Yul (Land of the Thunder Dragon)
(druhk-yool)

Capital: Thimphu

History

Bhutan—Between Two Giants

Bhutan is just north of India and just south of China. So you would think that people from these two great civilizations often visited the small nation between them. But that's not the case. Forbidding mountains in Bhutan's north and sticky jungles in its south have kept the country isolated until quite recently.

The first Bhutanese may have come from Tibet, a northern neighbor that China invaded and took over in the 1950s. Before the 1600s, most people lived around Bhutan's many *dzongs,* fort-like Buddhist monasteries still used today.

At least two early rulers in the country were monks. Records found in the monasteries show that a *lama,* or Buddhist monk, named Sheptoon La-Pha became king in about 1630. Bhutan's next king, Doopgein Sheptoon, was also a lama.

A Mountain Country

Since Bhutan is so mountainous, it was hard for the king to visit all parts of the kingdom. So Doopgein Sheptoon appointed governors for different regions. Unfortunately, these governors soon became as powerful as the king, and this resulted in several civil wars in the 19th century. In 1907, one of the governors, Ugyen Wangchuk, became king of the country.

The British controlled India throughout the 19th century. But Bhutan was so hard to travel to that the British didn't try to move directly into the tiny kingdom. Instead, they agreed to give money to Bhutan's government, beginning in 1865. In 1910, King Ugyen signed a treaty with Britain. He agreed that the British in India would guide Bhutan's dealings with other countries. Jigme Singye Wangchuk, Bhutan's present king, is the fourth king of Ugyen's line.

His father, Jigme Dorji Wangchuk, knew that the outside world was more advanced than his kingdom. So he began to introduce new economic, political, and social ideas, especially from India. Many Bhutanese had always looked to Tibet for religious guidance. They were not sure they wanted influence from India—or anywhere else outside Bhutan. But respect for the king prevented any serious flareup.

But the king himself may have thought there was too much influence coming from India. He had appointed a prime minister who wanted stronger ties between Bhutan and India. In 1969, the prime minister was shot to death. An army general was charged with the killing, but some people believe he acted under the king's orders. No one may ever really know what happened. King Jigme Dorji Wangchuk died in 1972, and the general was executed.

Bhutan's Army

The army has played an important part in Bhutan's recent history. When the Chinese took control of Tibet, the Bhutanese increased the size of their army. Even so, Bhutan's tiny army would stand little chance against the large Chinese army. Despite this, it still watches over the kingdom's cold, high northern border.

Today, Bhutan is a neutral country and a member of the United Nations. India, which gained independence from Britain in 1947, still guides and advises Bhutan's government according to an agreement signed in 1949. The agreement states that Bhutan will run its own internal affairs but that India will advise and guide it in dealings outside the country. India also gives Bhutan money. Recently, many Bhutanese have worked toward changing the agreement so that Bhutan has more freedom in its relations with other countries.

Government

Bhutan is a monarchy. That means it is ruled by a king. There is no constitution. Bhutan, in fact, may have been among the very last places on Earth to end slavery—serfdom was not outlawed until 1958! But Bhutan's government is slowly starting to recognize basic human rights.

The country is divided into four regions, each run by a governor whom the king appoints. Locally, each village has an elected headman.

The village headmen are part of Bhutan's court system. When people are accused of a crime or have a dispute, their cases are heard by the headmen or by *thrimpon,* or local judges. People who disagree with the headmen or thrimpon can appeal to Bhutan's six-member High Court, and finally, to the king himself. Most of Bhutan's laws are based on English and Indian law.

In making laws, a national assembly called the *Tsongdu* advises the king. It has a maximum of 150 members. There are no political parties, but the Bhutanese people elect as many as 100 assembly members from among their fellow citizens. Each family has one vote. The king appoints 40 others, and groups of lamas choose ten. Since 1969, the king has allowed the Tsongdu to veto, or refuse, proposed laws from him or his council.

In addition to the headmen and the Tsongdu, there are 12 more royal advisors. This group includes two Indians who advise Bhutan on economic affairs. Bhutan has no income tax, and its government spends more money than it takes in, so economic advice is vital!

Bhutan's government gets some money by accepting aid from other countries. It also makes a bit of money from tourists who are now allowed to visit if they are part of an approved tour. The government also makes some money by selling Bhutanese stamps, which collectors everywhere prize. These stamps are colorful miniature works of art. And they do not simply show interesting scenery or people. A stamp sold in the 1970s was a tiny record that played Bhutan's national anthem!

Currency

Bhutan's unit of currency is the *ngultrum,* which is equal to the Indian rupee. One ngultrum equals about eight cents in US currency. Delicate colors and detailed engravings make the money seem like art. Bhutanese paper currency is not very old. It was first issued in 1974, at the coronation of the king.

Languages

Most Bhutanese speak *Dzongkha,* a language that came from Tibet. The name shows that it probably was first used or introduced in the dzongs that dot Bhutan's countryside. Bhutan's other major language is Nepali, spoken by most of the Nepalese in Bhutan.

Population and Ethnic Groups

The current population of Bhutan is about 15 million. Most Asian countries have more people in each square mile of land. About 60% of Bhutan's people are Bhotias. These people have their roots in Tibet. Another 25% of Bhutan's people are Nepalese, and the remainder are small tribal groups, migrant workers, and laborers who have come to work and live in Bhutan.

The Bhotias

The Bhotias call themselves the *Drukpas,* or ''Dragon People.'' Many are farmers who live in large houses with high, thick walls of wood and tightly packed earth. Other houses are built of large bricks made of stone mixed with clay. Farm families often build their houses and other buildings close together. In the countryside, many families do not own a lot of furniture, except for a stove and a few chests for clothes and other important things.

Bhutan's marriages differ from those in many parts of the world. Women in some parts of Bhutan can have more than one husband. They can and do divorce with ease. This might be so because Bhutanese men are often gone for long periods when their animals need to graze in distant valleys. When husbands are home, they are expected to share equally in household duties. Men and women alike wear warm, bright woolen pants or robes.

The Nepalese

Almost all Bhotias practice a form of Tibetan Buddhism, while most Nepalese are Hindu. The Nepalese have been forbidden to move out of the southwest quarter of the kingdom into the central valleys where most Bhotias live. In recent years, the Nepalese in Bhutan have been trying to get the government to treat them equally, but the Bhotias want them kept where they are now. This causes friction between the two groups and the government, but things have stayed peaceful.

Like the Bhotias, the Nepalese often think of themselves more as members of their ethnic group than they might as citizens of Bhutan. Even as Bhutan becomes more modern in its ways, they have tried to keep their own traditions and ways of life. Most Bhotias live in a village that surrounds a dzong, while Nepalese are often found in villages along trade routes between Nepal or India and central Bhutan.

Religions

Most Bhutanese think about their religion every day. About a quarter of Bhutan's people are Hindu and about 5% are Muslims, Christians, and members of other faiths, including tribal religions. But about three out of four Bhutanese are Buddhists. Because of this, Buddhism can be called Bhutan's national religion. It touches the life of everyone in Bhutan.

Buddha — The Enlightened One

Buddhism began in India about 2,500 years ago with a man named Siddhartha Gautama, who is called the Buddha. Buddha means ''Enlightened One.'' As a young man, Buddha began trying to find how people could find peace, wisdom, and truth. He tried many different ways of life, but none of them seemed right.

According to one traditional Buddhist story, Buddha then saw an old man, a sick man, and a dead man. When this happened, he realized that all human beings must suffer in life.

Buddha thought about this for years. He started trying to understand why this was so, and wondered if people could find a way to end their suffering. Buddha, like many people in India both then and now, believed that all living beings are endlessly being born, living, and dying.

He came to believe that by living a good and right life, a person could escape this painful cycle, end his or her suffering, and become one with the universe.

The Noble Eightfold Path

Buddhists believe that people can end suffering by following what they call the Noble Eightfold Path. This path, which is really a way of life, consists of right ideas, right intentions, right speech, right actions, right work, right effort, right-mindedness, and right contemplation, or serious thinking about what is right.

Respect for Animal Life

Another basic idea in this religion is the belief that all life is sacred. Buddhists often turn to people of other faiths, such as Muslims, when livestock needs to be slaughtered. They will pay to have a yak or pig killed but will seldom butcher animals themselves. They are even reluctant to kill silkworms! Animals appear often as religious symbols in Tibetan Buddhism. So do dragons, demons, and various spirits.

Tibetan Buddhism

As Buddhism spread throughout Asia, the people who practiced it sometimes combined its teachings with their own traditions. Most Bhutanese follow a branch of Buddhism that was brought to the country hundreds of years ago from Tibet. This lamaistic Buddhism, or Buddhism as interpreted by lamas, or monks, is a blend of features from the original Buddhist religion from India and features from Himalayan culture.

Tibetan Buddhism began about 1,300 years ago. When the original Buddhist teachings first came to Tibet, the leaders of Tibet's native religion, Bon, tried to keep Buddhism from spreading. But the new faith became accepted under Tibetan kings who were Buddhists themselves. From about the 11th through the 13th centuries, Tibetan Buddhist lamas compiled and translated Buddhist scriptures. Many of these scriptures are the only versions that we now have of ancient Indian texts originally written in an old, old language called Sanskrit.

A rare animal, the takin, is protected by the king.

The Dalai Lama

There were many different groups, or sects, of lamas, each with their own special teachings. In the 15th century, one monk, Gan-den Trup-pa, became the head of a powerful sect called the Ge-luk-pa, or Yellow Hats. Later, he became the first Dalai Lama.

The Dalai Lama is the leader of Tibetan Buddhists everywhere and has been the head of Tibet's government. The current Dalai Lama is the 14th in Gan-den Trup-pa's line. He is no longer governing his country, however, because in 1959 he and other Buddhist leaders had to seek refuge in India, after the Chinese invaded Tibet.

The Hindu Nepalese

Most of the Nepalese in Bhutan are Hindus. Hinduism has hundreds of gods and symbols, but there is no one creed or set of beliefs that all Hindus share. Rather, Hindus choose the beliefs that are most meaningful to them. Hindus also believe there are different castes, or levels, and members of these castes have certain occupations. As Hindus, the Nepalese in Bhutan have higher and lower castes within their own group, but whatever their own caste may be, Nepalese in Bhutan consider themselves to be of a higher caste than the Bhotias. Despite this belief, the two groups seem to get along.

BHUTAN — Political and Physical

PEOPLE'S REPUBLIC OF CHINA

Nyamah

Tsona Dzong

H i m a l a y a s

Kula Gangri Changtsu
24,784 ft/7,435 m

Dangma

Bumtang

Tongsa

Tongsa Dzong

B H U T A N

Chomo Lhari 24,040 ft/7,212 m

Punakha

Lake Bamcho

Taga Dzong

Thimphu

Amo Chu

Paro Dzong

Ai

Brahmaputra

I N D I A

Someswari

Khasi Hills

Tura

Alipur Duar

Rangpur

T I B E T
[China]

H i m a l a y a s

Lake Kala

Kanchenjunga
28,208 ft/8,462 m

Darjeeling

Tista

NEPAL

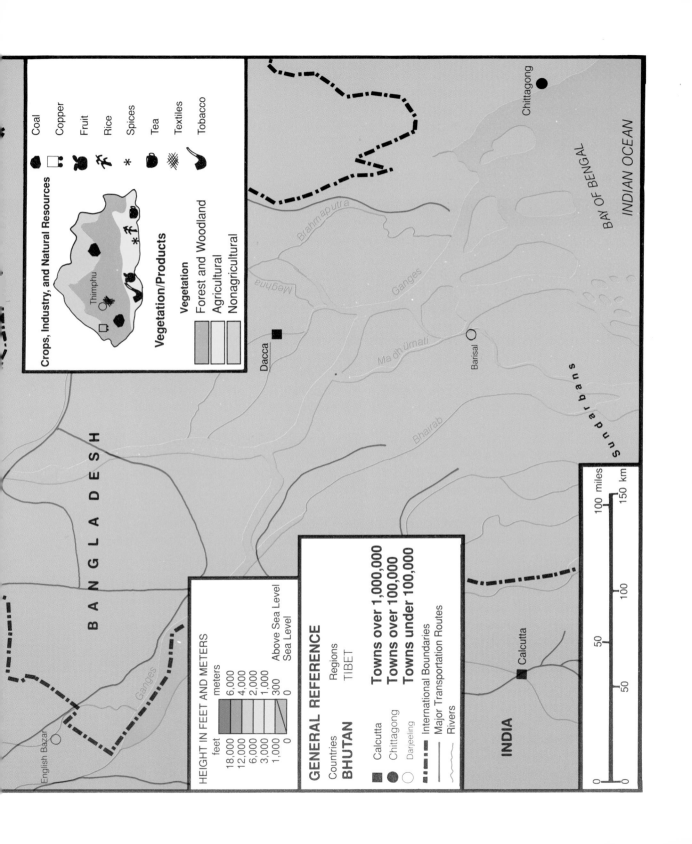

Crops, Industry, and Natural Resources

Coal	Copper
Fruit	Rice
Spices	Tea
Textiles	Tobacco

Thimphu

Vegetation/Products

Vegetation

Forest and Woodland
Agricultural
Nonagricultural

HEIGHT IN FEET AND METERS

feet	meters	
18,000	6,000	
12,000	4,000	
6,000	2,000	
3,000	1,000	
1,000	300	Above Sea Level
0	0	Sea Level

GENERAL REFERENCE

Countries   Regions
BHUTAN   TIBET

■ Calcutta   **Towns over 1,000,000**
● Chittagong   **Towns over 100,000**
○ Darjeeling   **Towns under 100,000**

International Boundaries
Major Transportation Routes
Rivers

BANGLADESH

Brahmaputra

Meghna

Ganges

Madhumati

Bhairab

Dacca

Barisal

Sundarbans

Chittagong

BAY OF BENGAL

INDIAN OCEAN

English Bazar

Ganges

INDIA

Calcutta

0	50	50	100	100 miles
0	50	100	150 km	

Land

Bhutan has about 18,000 square miles (46,000 sq km) of land. It is about the size of Vermont and New Hampshire together and slightly smaller than Nova Scotia. India wraps around Bhutan on the west, south, and east. To the north is China. The country has three main regions—the Great Himalayas, the Lesser Himalayas, and the Duars Plain.

The Himalayas

To understand Bhutan, its history, and its people, it helps to know a little about the Himalayas. This great Asian mountain range, which includes Mount Everest and several other high mountains, is the highest in the world.

The Himalayas stretch roughly from west to east about 1,560 miles (2,500 km), from northern Pakistan to eastern India. For centuries, the Himalayas have defined the northern borders of Bhutan and nearby Nepal.

These mountains have been very important in shaping Bhutan and its history. In many ways, the Himalayas have been one reason why Bhutan has been so isolated from the outside world. The mountains were, and still are, a barrier that is hard to cross on either side. But modern transportation is slowly making it easier to get through—and fly above—the steep passes and dangerous cliffs.

Because the mountains are so high and difficult for anyone to pass through, no one has ever really agreed as to exactly where Bhutan's northern border really is! As a result, Bhutan's government and China's government sometimes do not agree as to where their countries begin and end.

Some Chinese maps show parts of Bhutan as if they were parts of China. At times, Chinese soldiers have crossed into lands that Bhutan's government says are part of Bhutan. So Bhutan, with India's help, has been teaching its own soldiers how to fight in small groups in the mountains.

Bhutan—Three Small Countries in One

Bhutan might be small, but it has three very different kinds of land.

Bhutan's northern territory is in the Great Himalayas, snow-capped mountains as high as 24,000 feet (7,300 m) above sea level. Amid the mountains are valleys as deep as 18,000 feet (5,500 m) above sea level. People bring their yaks to graze in these valleys in the summer months, but there is little vegetation. No one lives there year-round.

Most Bhutanese live in valleys amid the Lesser Himalayas. These fertile valleys run from north to south and are less than 9,000 feet (2,740 m) above sea level. The mountains are spurs of the Great Himalayas. The rainy westward slopes are often covered with dense forest. On the drier eastward slopes are rocks and scrubby trees.

South of the mountains and some foothills is the Duars Plain. This area is only eight to ten miles wide (13 to 16 km) and runs along much of Bhutan's border with India. It is a hot, steamy, and unhealthy place, with forests, grasslands, and bamboo jungles. Elephants, deer, tigers, and other wild animals—including malaria-carrying mosquitoes—live here. Not many Bhutanese call this area home. They are slowly clearing some parts of this plain, however, so that they can grow crops.

Climate

For a small country, Bhutan has wide variations in climate. Along its southern border, 200 to 300 inches of rain (500 to 760 cm) fall each year. Far to the north, amid the Great Himalayas, are mountain peaks where the temperature never rises above freezing.

These rocky peaks don't get much snow, but they always have snow covering them. Temperatures throughout the year range from 100°F (38°C) or more in the lowland south to far below freezing atop northern mountains.

Between its border jungles and mountains, Bhutan has a livable, temperate climate. The fertile Lesser Himalaya mountain valleys receive rain from the southwest monsoon, a great wind that sweeps into Bhutan each summer.

Thimphu

Bhutan's capital and largest city, Thimphu, is in the western part of the country's Lesser Himalayas. At one time, Bhutan's government did its work from Thimphu only in the winter. The summer capital was Punakha, about 15 miles (24 km) northeast of Thimphu. The Bhutanese government came to Thimphu for the first time in 1955. In 1962, Thimphu became Bhutan's year-round capital.

Visitors to Bhutan often stay at the Motithang Hotel, high on a hill. From the hotel windows, people can look out over the entire valley. But many tourists want to go to the Bhutan Hotel, in downtown Thimphu. At this hotel, a guest might meet many different kinds of people, from high government officials to United Nations workers.

It is still not easy to get around in Bhutan, even in its biggest city. Bhutan does not have many modern highways, and there are no railroads leading to Thimphu. The closest airport is in Paro, about 15 miles (24 km) west of Thimphu. From there, it's a bus or car trip.

Thimphu, like the rest of Bhutan, is still not as modern as much of the rest of the world, but it has changed a lot in the last few years. As Bhutan becomes more like other modern countries, people who walk down Thimphu's streets see new stores and factories being built.

A Bhutanese airplane.

The mail service bus.

An old Indian Army truck.

Industry

Bhutan has no one major industry. But that does not mean that Bhutan's economic future is bleak. Its plunging rivers can be harnessed to generate electrical power. Since the Bhutanese consume little electricity, Bhutan could sell electric power to other countries. A major dam that produces power was recently completed and more new dams are being planned. Dam building, in fact, helped create a new industry in Bhutan—cement-making.

Cottage industries—handicraft businesses based in the home—are popular with tourists, who provide Bhutan with foreign currency. These handcrafted items include woolen cloth, leather goods, woven cotton and silk, wood carvings, bamboo baskets, paintings, silver jewelry, and jewelry made from things like yak hair.

The Bhutanese mine some semiprecious stones for jewelry to be sold within the country. Turquoise, amber, and coral beads are attractive—and bought quickly. Finally, stamp collectors all over the world trade in Bhutan's attractive and unusual postage stamps.

Agriculture

Agriculture is a basic part of life for most Bhutanese—most grow and preserve their own food. In warm weather, the men take yaks into high valleys to graze. During the winter, they drive the animals south toward lower elevations where there is more grass. Most Bhutanese live in villages in the central valleys.

Rice is Bhutan's main food. Two popular types are red rice and white rice. The red rice, which the Bhutanese prefer, is really pink. Bhutanese who eat meat consume yak, pork, and an occasional chicken. They serve meat with hot, spicy chili peppers. They also serve these peppers with other foods, such as corn, wheat, barley, onions, potatoes, fruit, and nuts. The people grow their food on small family plots surrounding villages or in valleys that they flood for rice paddies. Most Bhutanese have enough to eat, so the country is able to export some of its crops to India.

Natural Resources

Besides the semiprecious stones mined for jewelry, Bhutan is rich in forests. Many of these forests remain untouched, an untapped source of income. Thick pine and hardwood forests cover more than half of the country. Bhutan is one of the few countries in Asia that has not yet harvested many of its trees. This is partly because there are few good roads in Bhutan. Loggers need these roads to move their equipment into the forests and transport the logs to mills.

The rhododendron, the national flower.

Education

Education is free. But not all Bhutanese children go to school since Bhutan's school system is still developing. Perhaps, for the Bhutanese, this is fortunate, because many families still move about with livestock or live far from any school. If education were compulsory, it would be difficult for these people to get their children to school.

Those children who do go to school start at age six. There are about 140 elementary schools, 22 middle schools—which cover grades six through ten —and several high schools. Some Bhutanese attend technical schools and colleges or schools that specialize in training teachers.

Sports and Recreation

Bhutanese men and boys are proud of being first-rate archers. They do not shoot straight at a target, but fire their arrows in graceful, precise arcs above the mark so the arrows drop to the target.

The Bhutanese have few electronic forms of entertainment. Bhutan has its own radio stations, but no television stations. Even so, there are a few television sets and at least one video store in Thimphu.

Arts and Crafts

Bhutanese women pass on from generation to generation complicated woven designs. An adult female has a loom on which she weaves her fabric. Some pieces can take years to make. Even as she is weaving these beautiful art pieces, a woman continues to weave the cloth that will be used to make the family's clothes.

Many Bhutanese arts and crafts have a connection with Tibetan Buddhism. Through the years, the people have passed down colorful carved masks, many with a tiny skull atop them to frighten evil spirits away. During festivals, the people combine history, music, and dance. Dancers tell stories of courageous monks and great warriors to pounding drums and clashing cymbals.

Dancers design and make their own masks.

Much of the art comes from religion. When the Bhutanese enter their dzongs, they see the intricate, lustrous statues of Buddha. Throughout the dzongs are other beautiful carvings related to Buddhism. The Buddhist scriptures themselves are a form of art. They have been printed on hand-carved wooden blocks.

Bhutanese in North America

Very few Bhutanese have entered North America. From 1978 until 1984, only seven had come into Canada, and these were students who undoubtedly returned to Bhutan. About 72 students entered the US from 1978 until 1986. Around 100 Bhutanese come to the US each year as visitors—government officials, businesspeople, and vacationers. Bhutan is just opening up to the West, which may account for such low numbers of Bhutanese travelers.

More Books About Bhutan

The Himalayas. Nicolson (Time-Life)
The Story of Buddha. Landaw (Auromere)
A Way of the Buddha. Burland (Dufour)

Glossary of Useful Bhutanese Terms

aiee (EYE-ee) . . . . mother
apa (AH-pah) . . . . father

dzong (dzahng). . . . . temple

ema-datzy (A-mah-daht-ZEE) . . . . pepper cheese, a Bhutanese national dish

goh (go) . . . . a traditional piece of clothing for men and boys

kadin-che (kah-DIN-chay) . . . . thank you

kamni (KAHM-nee) . . . . a piece of cloth men wear over their shoulders

kira (KEY-rah) . . . . a jumper-like piece of clothing for women and girls

kuzuzhangpo (KOO-zoo-zohng-poh) . . . . hello

lobda (LOWB-dah) . . . . school

logjegay (LOG-jay-gay). . . . . good-bye

lopon (LOW-pahn). teacher

Things to Do—Research Projects

Today the leader of the Buddhists, the Dalai Lama, is outside his native country, Tibetan China, and speaking to the rest of the world about world peace. He has been nominated for the Nobel Peace Prize and many believe he will earn it one day. As you read about the Dalai Lama, keep in mind the importance of current facts. Some of the research projects that follow need accurate, up-to-date information. That is why current newspapers and magazines are useful sources of information. Two publications your library may have will tell you about recent magazine and newspaper articles on many topics:

Readers' Guide to Periodical Literature
Children's Magazine Guide

For accurate answers to questions about such topics of current interest as the Dalai Lama, look up *Dalai Lama* in one of these publications. They will lead you to up-to-date information.

Here are other projects:

1. Bhutan and China continue to skirmish near the northern border of Bhutan. Learn more about the relations between these long-time neighbors.

2. The Himalayas give Bhutan much of its beauty but they also make great demands on the people who live near them. Learn more about these mountains and the lives of the people who live in and near them.

3. How far is Thimphu from where you live? Can you find an overland route to the city? What airlines go into or near the city? Using maps, travel guides, travel agents, or any other resources you know of, find out how you could get to Thimphu and how long your journey might take.

More Things to Do—Activities

1. Learn more about Buddhist religious days. With a group of friends or classmates, plan a religious festival. Try to learn why this holiday is important, what foods might be served, and what rituals the people perform.

2. How does your life compare to Tinley's? Write an imaginary letter to him. Explain the ways in which you might be similar and the ways that you are different.

3. If you would like a pen pal in Bhutan, write to these people:

International Pen Friends
P.O. Box 290065
Brooklyn, NY 11229-0001

Worldwide Pen Friends
P. O. Box 6896
Thousand Oaks, CA 91359

Be sure to tell them what country you want your pen pal to be from. Also include your full name and address.

Goodbye from the Land of the Thunder Dragon.

Index